SPOKEN WORSHIP

SPOKEN WORSHIP

LIVING WORDS *for* PERSONAL AND PUBLIC PRAYER

GERARD KELLY

ZONDERVAN.com/
AUTHORTRACKER
follow your favorite authors

ZONDERVAN®

Spoken Worship
Copyright © 2007 by Gerard Kelly

Requests for information should be addressed to:

Zondervan, *Grand Rapids, Michigan* 49530

Gerard Kelly asserts the moral right to be identified as the author of this work.

Library of Congress Cataloging-in-Publication Data

Kelly, Gerard, 1959 –.
    Spoken worship / Gerard Kelly.
      p. cm.
    Includes bibliographical references and index [if applicable].
    ISBN-10: 0-310-27550-4
    ISBN-13: 978-0-310-27550-3
    1. Liturgies. 2. Public worship. I. Title.
BV198.K45 2007
264 – dc22   2006037559

Interior design by Melissa Elenbaas

Printed in the United Kingdom

---

07 08 09 10 11 • 10 9 8 7 6 5 4 3 2 1

For Rob Lacey,
poet, actor, friend
and co-conspirator
In memoriam

We have only the word, but the word will do. It will do because it is true that the poem shakes the empire, that the poem heals and transforms and rescues, that the poem enters like a thief in the night and gives new life, fresh from the word and from nowhere else. There are many pressures to quiet the text, to silence this deposit of dangerous speech, to halt this outrageous practice of speaking alternative possibility. The poems, however, refuse such silence. They will sound. They sound through preachers who risk beyond prose. In the act of such risk, power is released, newness is evoked, God is praised.

– WALTER BRUEGGEMANN,
FINALLY COMES THE POET

Contents

Savour the Story

Psalm Enchanted Evening

Seasoning for the Seasons

Mystery Making

Introduction

spoken *adj* **1** *uttered or expressed in speech.* ETYMOLOGY: *Anglo-Saxon* specan.

worship *noun* **1 a** *the activity of worshipping;* **b** *the worship itself.* **2** *a religious service in which God or a god is honoured • morning worship.* ETYMOLOGY: *Anglo-Saxon* weorthscipe, *meaning 'worthship'.*

Spoken worship. Is it poetry? Is it prophecy? Is it prayer? Yes, yes and, in a sense, yes. Spoken worship is about the power of the spoken word to illumine human experience in the place where it matters most: connection to our creator. For centuries Christian worshippers from formal hymn-singing traditionalists to chandelier-swinging charismatics have set words to music to enhance the worship experience. In gatherings large and small, in great halls and home groups, in the shower before breakfast and in the car on the way to work, we sing our praises to God. But in doing so, have we forgotten the power of words spoken?

It's not that there's anything wrong with setting words to music and singing them. When it is done well – and it is often done well in our churches – it moves us and shapes us and stirs our hearts to action. But in twenty years of contributing to some of the largest Christian gatherings in Europe, I have discovered a little-known secret. I have discovered that the spoken word has a power of a different order of magnitude from the power of a word set to music. I have found that there is a special additional *something*, a deepening of the impact, when words are spoken into the holy space that is worship. This new form of poetry, spoken worship, forged in the shared experience of the gathered church, sits happily alongside 'the musical expression of worship' to bring richness and vigour to the devotional life of God's people.

And it doesn't belong only in the cathedrals of gathered worship. The real beauty of spoken worship is that it doesn't demand economies of scale. Poems written for worship in this way can be used in the largest of Christian gatherings. Many of the poems included in this collection have already been used in such gatherings, and some have been broadcast on radio and TV to 'congregations' in their millions. But they don't *need* the big crowd. They are just as at home in the small group, the one-to-one prayer time and the individual devotional life. That's the great secret of spoken worship: it's a carry-anywhere, use-everywhere medium. All you need is a pocket or a handbag with room for a small book, or a brain with room for memorised verse, and you can carry this worship experience everywhere you go. In this age of smart phones and pocket computers, it's even easier. You can carry a cathedral-sized worship resource in a pocket-sized device. Whether performed before a crowd of thousands or read quietly to that one patient whose stay in hospital has become a burden almost too heavy to bear, these pieces are a resource to worship wherever it is needed.

I believe there is vast potential for God's people to rediscover the power of the spoken word as a vital element in worship. If the pieces in this collection are a step in that direction, it will have been worth printing them. And it will be a still better outcome if the pieces in this collection prove a challenge and a stimulus for others to write their own spoken-worship pieces, and for the very many writers huddled in the closets of churches up and down the country to come out and get writing.

I wrote a piece for a workshop at the UK Soul Survivor Festival some years ago that began with the lines, "It's a coming-out party for closet poets." It was and is my dream to see more people realising just how gifted they are: that God has given them a voice and the words with which to fill it.

Spoken worship is, at its most basic, worship that is spoken. It has no official definition, but in essence it is poetry written for the context of Christian worship. It is writing whose ultimate goal is not so much literary as devotional, writing aimed unashamedly at provoking and prodding the human heart to wonder before its maker. Like many other forms of poetry, it is writing that has a life on the page but whose real life emerges only in performance: writing designed to be clothed in the human voice. Poet Dylan Thomas once observed that 'a poem on the page is only half a poem,' and many of these pieces, too, will be 'complete' only when they are read aloud. They try to find words that can capture and carry the love and longings of the heart of worship, and that can do so on behalf of others. They can be, I believe, an important and valuable tool in our worship toolbox.

Dylan Thomas rehearsed the first cast of his 'play for voices' *Under Milkwood* in New York in 1953. The piece was barely finished – Thomas was still scribbling lines and passing them to the actors on the day before the opening performance. He was exhausted and stressed, barely able to focus. But photographer Rollie McKenna remembers that at the final rehearsal, with no time left to iron out the imperfections in the performance, Thomas was alert and animated and saying to his actors over and over again, 'Love the words ... love the words'.

This is the calling, I believe, of the worship poet: to love words, and in words to carry love. Whatever else worship is, it is a language of the human heart. It speaks of deep longings, of love deeply felt, of ultimate concerns. Spoken worship allows worship to do so with new eloquence and depth. It is poetry of the soul, reaching out to the soul's greatest lover. Where deep calls to deep, spoken worship heeds the call.

– GERARD KELLY

Rob's God

For Rob Lacey

I want to follow Rob's God;
God the goal of my soul's education.
Rob's God is approachable, articulate and artful,
a glowing God
of graceful inclination.

Rob's God snowboards cloudscapes
and paints daisies on his toes
while watching Chaplin reruns on his iPod.
He smiles at cats and children,
jumps in puddles
with his shoes on;
he is a 'where's the fun in fundamentalism?' God.

Rob's God doesn't shoot
his wounded
or blame the poor for failing
at prosperity.
He doesn't beat the broken
with bruised reeds from their garden
or tell the sick that healing's
their responsibility.

Rob's God is a poet,
painting people as his poems;
a sculptor shaping symphonies from stone;

a maker of mosaics,
curator of collages
woven from the wounds and wonders
we have known.

A furnace of forgiveness,
Rob's God radiates reunion,
pouring oil on every fight
we've ever started;
a living lover
loving laughter,
lending light
to the helpless and the harmed and heavyhearted.

Other Gods may claim more crowded churches,
higher profiles,
better ratings,
fuller phone-ins,
but in the contest for commitment,
in the battle for belief,
in the war to woo my worship,
Rob's God wins.
In the fight for my faith's fervour,
in the struggle for my soul,
in the race for my respect,
Rob's God wins.

Absolutely.

THE BARRED BARD

Performance Notes

One of my all-time favourite characters in fiction is Cacophonix, the unfortunate bard featured in the adventures of Asterix and Obelix. Unfortunate because Cacophonix is blessed with an almost miraculous inability to sing. His compositions – long and tedious and peppered with pretentious and pompous language – are utterly hated by the very villagers whose joys and jubilations he extols. Every Asterix adventure I have read ends with the villagers enjoying a traditional 'now that the fighting is over we can get back to eating' feast, but with the hapless Cacophonix trussed up and gagged: the only guarantee of a much-needed silence.

For all the comedy value of the barred bard, I love the image of Cacophonix because he is the best illustration I know of, in contemporary culture, of the bardic calling. Where else is captured for us such a clear understanding of the essential role and function of the bard: to reflect in poetry and song the feelings, experiences, triumphs and tragedies through which the tribe have lately lived? The bard is a sounding board to the villagers he serves. He has a way with words, and perhaps music, that they do not, but the building blocks from which his performance is carefully constructed are drawn from the people themselves. They fight and win a war: he sings their victory back to them. They suffer and survive a plague: he recites their terrors and their triumph. They lose loved ones: he articulates the mourning of their corporate loss. In bardic art a two-way transaction takes place. The feelings of the people become the feelings of the poet, and the words of the poet become the words of the people. It is this transaction that marks out the most significant and distinct characteristic of worship poetry: it is poetry spoken on behalf of others.

Where much contemporary poetry restricts itself to – indeed prides itself on – the exposure of the private feelings of an individual, spoken worship does not. Worship is by definition a shared experience: it is the response of a community to God its creator. Even when she worships alone, the worshipper stands in radical solidarity with the family of God through space and time. She is, as Wordsworth noted, 'never less alone than when alone'. Worship is not a private, obscure, barely intelligible transaction between a God lost in the clouds and a seeker lost in confusion;

it is an expression born in belonging, a shared articulation of the human touching the divine. Spoken worship, then, cannot afford to be written in a private code; it does not dare to be obscure. It must, rather, touch the depth of the meaning of worship in such a way that those who hear it, or read it, or themselves speak it out, are drawn into the experience. It may be a secret garden into which the traveller has never before strayed, but it must be a garden whose blooms, once found, are recognised as such. It speaks to the heart and the heart knows its voice.

This does not mean that spoken worship must be bland – that it must speak in the language of a menu at McDonald's. To be accessible and intelligible is not, by definition, to be shallow, and unless spoken worship is in some way deep – unless it goes somewhere that those engaging in it would not otherwise go – it has nothing to offer. It must live in the tension between obscurity and banality, between indecipherable depth and unpalatable shallowness. Somehow, spoken worship must take deep things and make them accessible. Its goal is resonance, that beautiful moment of connection when a worshipper can say, 'I feel this too, I just didn't know how to say it.'

The worship poet, then, has a responsibility far beyond the existential call to 'know thyself'. She must know herself because words that are not authentic to their writer cannot, with any real depth, be meaningful to others. But self-knowledge and self-expression are not enough. She must also have the power and the willingness to listen, to know others, to sense and experience and explore and express and respond to *their* aspirations and expectations. Spoken worship is poetry written for others – on their behalf and for their participation.

It follows, then, that the gift most essential to the creation of spoken worship is the gift of empathy, and time and energy invested in this gift will be richly rewarded when it comes to both the composition and the delivery of spoken worship. Without this gift, the most finely crafted piece will have no power; with it even a few stuttered and stumbling words can play their part. Before even putting pen to paper or stepping up to a mike, an indispensable principle must be embraced: learn to listen, and listen to learn. This is the craft of the worship poet. Spoken worship is a mirror held up to those who seek God. As well as polishing the words and their delivery, there is much to be said for polishing the mirror.

The Blessing

May you who are restless
find rest,
and in rest, restoration
and the healing
of your hollow soul.
May peace be yours.

May you who are frozen
find freedom,
and in freedom, the strength
to face the fire
and the thawing
of your ice-gripped heart.
May peace be yours.

May you who are conflicted
find convergence,
and in convergence, confidence
to be the one new child
of your old divided self.
May peace be yours.

May you who live in tension
find tenderness,
and in tenderness, the tendency
to kindness
and the miracle

of majoring in mercy.
May peace be yours.

And you who are God-less,
may you find God,
and in God,
the grace and growth you need
for fruit and fullness
and the love that will last you
through the long haul
of a lived-for-others life.
May peace be yours.

Blindness and Sight

When we claim to have foresight,
second sight
and insight
when in reality
even our first sight is short:
Father, open our eyes.

When we blunder on blindly
like ships in dense fog,
never knowing
how lost we truly are,
never seeing
past the end of our needs:
Father, open our eyes.

When we collide with one another
like bats with malfunctioning radar,
not even noticing
the damage we have done:
Father, open our eyes.

When we walk through your world
as if we ourselves
had made it
and fail to recognise
the fingerprints you leave:
Father, open our eyes.

When we are blind to your presence
in the eyes of the poor,
blind to the perfection
that lies visibly before us,
blind to your handiwork,
blind to your care,
blind to the signs
that you scatter all around us:
Father, heal our sight.

Worth-ship

For you I'd join
a mariachi band
and make such music
that the stones themselves would dance
and shout your name, their joy a flame
to melt the hardness
of a frost-gripped land.
For you.

For you I'd mould
a papier-mâché world
and spin the globe,
a blur of blue and green,
a marvellous, marbled sight: alive with light,
creation's boundless beauties
free, unfurled.
For you.

For you I'd fold
an origami temple,
a newsprint palace,
a tabloid Taj Mahal,
an onion field of whispering domes
to echo love's remembered songs,
a 'Hallelujah Chorus'
in each line.
For you.

For you I'd fly
the flags of all the nations,
a sky-wide surge
of many-coloured silk,
a floating, fabric ocean: breath in motion,
unspoken words
in waves of celebration.
For you.

And for you I'd walk
a thousand weary roads
and step by step
push on in perseverance,
pursuing paths of purpose: in ordinary kindness,
I'd daily find my cross
and bear its load.
For you.

This servant life,
this gift of giving,
this halo of help
held out to the hopeless,
this love
my firm
and final act of worship.
For you.

One

Though the skins that are stretched over us
have shades enough
to mark a path from coal to snow
in micron increments,
we are one.

Though the fine lines of our features
are freehand enough
that even smiles
are signatures of difference,
we are one.

Though the cultures that encode us
are cryptic enough
to make each one of us a mystery to the other,
we are one.
Though the polarities that plague us
can have power enough
to make sparks fly
every time we come together,
we are one.

Though the stories that have shaped us
are self-penned enough
to fill a library with the secrets we each hide,
and though the route maps we rely on
may be rough enough

to make finding common ground
a roller-coaster ride;
though the distinctives that define us
may be deep enough
to aggravate and irritate and painfully divide,
and though the languages we vocalise
are localised enough
to keep a truckload of translators tongue-tied,
we are one.

Many: but one.
Different: but one.
Awkward: but one.
Reluctant: but one.
Taught: to be one,
bar none.
May our maker
make us one.

Glad

I'm glad that God
did not so order the world
that laughter and pain
come in separate little boxes,
never to meet
or mingle.

I'm glad that the greatest of comedians
can bring me to the verge of despair,
and that a quadriplegic
who paints with his teeth
and taps out prose
one letter at a time
can remind me
of the richness of comedy.

I'm glad that laughter and pain
come intertwined
like veins in marble
and that it takes a detective
to trace them
and poems
to root them out.

Elemental

You catch us when our heart is fading.
You warm us when our love is cooling.
You ignite us,
enlighten us,
consume us,
refine us.
You are fire
and we welcome your flame.

You fill the space we make for you.
You shape the lives immersed in you.
You cleanse us,
refresh us,
flow through us,
renew us.
You are water
and we submit to your tide.

You feed the seeds we plant in you.
You strengthen roots laid deep in you.
You hold us,
sustain us,
nourish us,
bring life to us.
You are earth
and in you we ground our being.

You fill the lungs of those who draw on you.
You fill the sails of those who wait for you.
You carry us,
move us,
lift us,
caress us.
You are air
and to breathe of you is life.

Burn us, fire of heaven;
wash us, holy water;
grow us, ground of our being;
inspire us, breath of God.
Remake us, great Creator,
in your elemental image.

THE POWER OF THE POEM

Performance Notes

The great British writer C. S. Lewis became a Christian when he understood that his lifelong search for joy was in fact a search for God. Joy, to Lewis, was the unattainable desire that would surface in unexpected times and places, calling him to contemplate the perfection of beauty. He later labelled it 'aesthetic experience', but even in doing so, he knew the words were not enough. Joy was for the deepest moments of life, the purest experiences of primal beauty. All his adult life Lewis searched for such moments and wondered what their true source might be.

But if the discovery of God marked the end of this great search for Lewis, it was the discovery of poetry that began it. As a boy Lewis had become a fan of the poetry of Henry Wadsworth Longfellow, though his interest was rarely more than casual. Until one day he turned a page to discover the poem 'Tegner's Drapa' and its opening words:

> I heard a voice that cried,
> Balder the beautiful
> Is dead, is dead....[1]

Lewis knew nothing about Balder, but something in these words went to the very depths of his soul. He was uplifted, drawn somehow, to the rare beauty of the northern skies and the pale and remote intensity that gave birth to the epic tales of Norse mythology. This shaft from the great beyond, this glimpse of joy, was enough to set the young Lewis on a lifelong journey in search of the source of such beauty. Not until he found his satisfaction in the bosom of a loving God was Lewis able to relax his constant searching. Such is the power of poetry. A few words arranged in a particular way and the quest for faith is awakened in one of the greatest minds of his generation.

What is to be learned from this for the worship poet of today? Only that it is impossible to overstate the potential power of poetry. For the right person, at the right moment, in the right situation, a single phrase can be enough to awaken longings that a lifetime will not fulfil. Poetry has the power to open avenues other forms of discourse have left closed. It can melt the locks on perception and swing wide the gates of exploration. It can be a call to higher aspirations, an invitation to the deepest rivers of desire.

Language has always been the vehicle of the human imagination. It is our capacity to speak – and to transfer conceptual thinking by means of words from one mind to another – that sets us apart from our fellow creatures. Every achievement of human history is ultimately an achievement of words. Every new door is opened by the power of words. Words make us what we are. The best of what we will be, we will be by the power of words. But we live all too often, as Walter Brueggemann insists, in a prose world: a world 'organised in settled formulae, so that even pastoral prayers and love letters sound like memos'.[2] In order to address such a world, to combat the reduction of truth and awaken the human spirit to surprise, we must be 'poets that speak against a prose world'.[3] Poetry holds a mirror up to the best and the worst in us. It invites us to choose beauty over indifference, passion over indolence. It jump-starts the imagination when cold foggy mornings have left it asleep and snoring. And in poetry, words come dressed for dancing. They come gracefully, powerfully, directing themselves to the very centre of who we are.

Words can wound, but they can also heal. They can break down, but they can also build up. Words can be cruel and scathing, lashing with malice those who hear them. But they can also be uplifting. They can speak beauty into places of ugliness and hope into the darkness of despair.

Never underestimate the power of a poem. You never know what journeys the reading of it may begin.

The Games People Pray

Some pray like a BMW:
seven coats
of shine and shimmer
masking
the hardness of steel,
with an anti-emotion warranty
to guard against
the least sign of trust.

Some pray like a Porsche:
nought to victory
in 6.7 seconds,
banking on the promises
of pray-as-you-earn prosperity.

Jesus recommended praying
in the garage
with the door shut
and the radio off,
praying when no one is looking,
forgetting
the traffic of the day,
preferring
the quiet lay-by
to the clamour
of the Pray and Display.

The Taming of the Truth

Like a football match
where the fans are locked out
while the players take turns
on the terraces
to cheer,

like a concert
where the crowd sits in silence
while the band
play through headphones
so that only they hear.

Like a hospital
that keeps itself
germ-free and sterile
by treating only patients
who aren't sick,

like a spoonful of sugar
with no medicine,
like a mule
without a kick.

Like an ocean liner
on a pleasure cruise
purely for the pleasure
of the crew,

we have taken what was given
as a message for the many
and made of it
a massage
for the few.

I Choose to Forgive

Though the cuffs of my jeans are muddied
from the dirt you have dragged me through,
I choose to forgive.

Though the nails of my fingers are bloodied
from the fighting you've forced me to do,
I choose to forgive.

Though no book or belief I have studied
can make sense of the path you pursue,
I choose to forgive.

Though the walls of my heart are broken
and the centre of my self is black-bruised
by the lash of the lies that you've spoken
and the wounds of the words that you've used,
though I huddle, a tear-trembling tragedy
stripped of the power to trust,
blocked off from all who might help me
by the guilt that came wrapped with your lust,
I choose to forgive.

And this act alone
breaks the cycle.
This act alone
rights the wrong.
This act alone

ends the evil.
This act alone
makes me strong,

heals blind hatred with soft sight,
kicks the darkness into light.

I choose to forgive.

Stop the Traffic

I am a person,
not a potato
to be picked and packaged
and sent to market
to be sliced and diced,
chopped up and ketchupped
on the other side of the world.

I am human
and I am not for sale.

I am a living conscience,
not a cargo.
I travel passenger,
not freight.
I am not cattle,
not contraband,
not a catalogued commodity.
I'm not the bottom line
for those who trade in tragedy
and profit from perversity.
I am not a can
to be recycled.

I am human
and I am not for sale.

I am a thinking individual,
not a rare exotic bird.
I am your sister,
not an inmate for your zoo.
I am not merchandise,
not meat,
not a meal ticket.
I was mothered,
not manufactured,
begotten,
not created.

I am human
and I am not for sale.

It's time to end this trade
in human tragedy,
to terminate this travesty
of a global economy.
Let the red lights
of your cities
be put to better use
to stop the traffic.
Write it in lights
across your seared conscience:

I am human
and I am not for sale.

Fit Me In Somewhere

Fit me in somewhere
in this giant jigsaw, God,
somewhere in this work of art
you're working,
select a space my shape can fill
and with a puzzle maker's skill
let my contours find their fit without contortion.

Teach me which patch I am, God,
in the cosmic quilt you're quilting.
Show me where my square of selfhood is of use.
Let the colourful complexities
of the pattern that is me
find their purpose in the placement that you choose.

Show me my position, God,
in this group photograph.
Stand me where you want me to stand.
Put me next to whom you will.
Make me stand, for good or ill,
precisely in the place your plan demands.

Tell me what I am, God,
in this body you are building:
a tongue to taste,
a nerve to serve,
an ear to hear.

Give me grace
to not be, gracefully,
the parts I am not called to be
and to play with elegance
the roles I'm given.

Fit me in somewhere
in this giant jigsaw, God,
somewhere in this work of art you're working.
Weave your wondrous tapestry
until the twisted, tangled threads of me,
surrendered to your artistry,
form an image that is beautiful to see.

I Got Rhythm

Performance Notes

There is a simple rule about performance poetry that many would-be poets miss but no experienced performer will contest: not all poems rhyme, but every poem has rhythm. Rhythm is the heart and soul of poetry, and without rhythm, spoken worship has no right to waste our time. Even when rhyme is also used, rhyme cannot and must not take the place of rhythm, and in a standoff between the two, it is always the rhythm that must win.

It is difficult to explain just how the rhythmic quality of words works, but the difference between a performance that honours the rhythm of the words and a performance that does not can be heard by even a novice listener. The performance of Shakespeare week by week in theatres across the world proves this. The average passage of Shakespeare, read verbatim by the average reader, is barely intelligible. Most of us find it almost impossible to enjoy on the page. But the same passage spoken by a gifted actor, who has lived and breathed the text for months and has found the heart of its drama, becomes an exhilarating and poignant experience.

I have tested this three times with my children. As each of the three oldest has passed through their teenage years, we have together watched Baz Luhrmann's remarkable 1995 adaptation of *Romeo and Juliet*. Luhrmann leaves the script pretty much as is; the words his cast speak are the words of Shakespeare. But everything else changes – the setting, the props, the costumes and, most importantly, the intonation of the actors. By giving the play a modern/postmodern setting, Luhrmann empowers his actors to speak ancient words in a contemporary context. Two quite astounding examples stand out. The prologue to the play is read as a TV newscast – an insightful choice of the contemporary equivalent of Shakespeare's intent. The result is that as actress Edwina Moore reads these opening words with the dry delivery of a TV anchorwoman, their meaning becomes exponentially clearer.

Two households, both alike in dignity in fair Verona, where we lay our scene. From ancient grudge break to new mutiny where civil blood makes civile hands unclean. From forth the faital loins of these two foes a pair of star-cross'd lovers take their life; whose misadventured piteous overthrows doth with their death bury their parents' strife. The fearful passage of their reath-mark'd love and the continuance of their parents' rage which but their children's end nought could remove is now the two hours' traffic of our stage.

Equally, when Vondie Curtis-Hall, as Captain Prince, threatens the warring families with the sanction of the law and in due course banishes Romeo from the city, he does so with the intonation of a contemporary Police Captain, and the meaning of the words is once more made clear. Pete Postlethwaite, as Father Lawrence, captures in both voice and face the subtleties of an adult friend concerned to both help and somehow protect the young Romeo.

With every speech the inner drama of Romeo and Juliet became clearer and clearer to my teenage children and, as a bonus, to me.

The example of Shakespeare brings out the two principles that should guide the search for rhythm in the performance of poetry.

The first is that the rhythm is in the words, not in their metre. Metre has an important function in certain poems, but its role is not to dictate the pace or rhythm of performance. Poetry which is read with the metre, rather than the words, dictating rhythm becomes doggerel. This is why many poets, surprisingly, make poor songwriters. A choice must be made between the rhythm dictated by the tune, and hence by the metre, and the rhythm inherent in the words. It is this second road that the performance poet must follow, and finding it requires great skill and practise. Singers can do violence to the inherent rhythm of words in order to 'fit them' to a tune: poets cannot. They must both write and perform with a respect for the words they are using and let the rhythm of the performance flow from them.

The second principle is that rhythm is closely tied to meaning. It is the intent of the language that tells us how to read it. We reveal our understanding of the meaning of a phrase by the rhythm with which we read it. Flat, droning metre is not enough: it shows that we have read the words themselves but have not even tried to grasp their meaning. Rhythm, which includes timing, pace and the use of silence, will often do as much to convey meaning as the actual choice of words. Rhythm can communicate urgency, wonder, laughter, joy, emphasis, passion, pain, confusion, fear, acceptance, pleasure. The experience of spoken worship is derived not from the words alone but from the words and the voice together. An old proverb says that 'the light of a candle is neither in the wax, nor in the wick, but in the burning'. So it is with spoken worship. The words alone are not enough, and the voice alone has nothing to convey. But the voice creatively harnessed to give flight to the words can have real power.

Don't be satisfied with knowing, or thinking you know, the metre. Find the rhythm. Find the pace and flow which will unlock the meaning of the words you are speaking. Love the words and the spaces between the words. Learn to handle timing like a gymnast. Practise the graceful perfection of a good landing. Enjoy the 'aha' moments that come when well-chosen words are spoken by a well-trained voice.

Metre can often be the straightjacket that prevents words from speaking their truth. Rhythm, by contrast, is the freedom of the dance.

Liturgy: Let Your Kingdom Come

Let it break out like blisters
on the skin of this city.
Let it cut to the heart
like cardiac surgery.
Let it create more column inches
than *Idols* and *Big Brother.*
Let it turn more heads in public
than Brooklyn Beckham's mother.

Let it blow in like a hurricane,
like a river, like a fire.
Let it spread like a virus,
like a rumour, like a war.
Like the raising of a curtain,
like the roll of a drum,
let it come to us:
let your kingdom come.

Let its landing be more welcomed
than the Dalai Lama's jet.
Let it touch more homes and households
than the rise of credit debt.
Let it be prized as a possession
like a ball signed by Babe Ruth.
Let it take more liberties with hate
than the tabloids take with truth.

Let it hit the road more readily
than Eddie Stobart's trucks.
Let it show up in more suburbs
than Blockbuster and Starbucks.
Let it overturn more social norms
than Marge and Homer's Bart.
Let it be driven to more victories
than Tiger Woods' golf cart.

Let it blow in like a hurricane,
like a river, like a fire.
Let it spread like a virus,
like a rumour, like a war.
Like the raising of a curtain,
like the roll of a drum,
let it come to us:
let your kingdom come.

Let it sing a softer love song
than Chris de Burgh's red lady.
Let it blast out through more ghettoes
than Eminem's *Slim Shady*.
Let it win more public plaudits
than the acting of Tom Cruise.
Let it hold out hope for longer
than Disney's theme-park queues.

Let it pack more power potential
than a phone box with Clark Kent in.
Let it set more captives free
than a breakout at San Quentin.
Let it flow into as many lives
as water fluoridation.
Let it soak the soil more deeply
than Chernobyl's radiation.

Let it blow in like a hurricane,
like a river, like a fire.
Let it spread like a virus,
like a rumour, like a war.
Like the raising of a curtain,
like the roll of a drum,
let it come to us:
let your kingdom come.

Performance for an Audience of One

If you had been the only one,
yours the only ticket sold,
your solitary bottom
spoilt for choice
in an ocean of empty seats;
if you had been
the only one,
he still would have staged
the whole show.
The brooding, hovering chords
of the overture
unfolding
for your ears only:
stars spinning out like Catherine wheels
across a dark but lightening set
until dawn was uncorked
on green home.

Act 1: the building of a nation,
a people wooed and won
and lost
and won again,
for you alone the whole cast
weaving and turning through dances
to fill a joyous expanse of stage.

Act 2: the cry of a child
in a vastly empty universe,
the adventure of hope and betrayal,
the seat-gripping climax:
triumph's death-defying dive,
through the fiery hoop of tragedy.
The clamour of the crowd scenes
building
toward an unimagined finale:
a cosmos, purged of guilt,
restored,
dressed for dancing.

If you had been the only one,
your grimy pounds
the total take,
he still would have staged
the whole show
and wept for joy
at the warmth
of your applause.

Gimme Gimme Gimme Temptation

Like a microwave oven,
it starts to cook
on the inside.
Like the small ads
in the tabloids,
it offers
what it can't provide.

Like queues on the M25,
it brings the best plans
to a halt.
Like a badly brought up tennis star,
it never admits
to a fault.

Like a book club
joined in error,
it won't let you rest
'til you're dead.
Like a topless liquidizer,
its effects
are quickly widespread.

Like cut-price plastic surgery,
its after
is worse than its before.
Like any well-managed pop star,

it always leaves you
wanting more.

Like the shepherd's red sky at night,
it promises delight
at sunrise,
but
like the sleeping dog that it is,

it lies.

Mother's Song

I give you the earth,
my child, gift of love,
its contoured face carved
by time and the weather's knife,
its patchwork of forests
sewn with the threads of rivers,
its oceans
of salted life.

I give you the rhythms
of time and tide and voices,
the drumroll of rainfall
when the ground's tight skin is dry.
I give you a choir
of leaves to sing the wind to you,
a palette of sungold
for a canvassful of sky.

I give you your place
on this planet of wonders,
crown jewel of the heavens
in a Guinness-black dome.
I give you the garden
God's artistry has landscaped
to be your classroom and playground,
your palace,
your home.

For joy
I give you laughter.
For peace
I give you sleep.
For fear and failure,
my embrace to call upon.
I give you the earth,
my child, gift of love,
and I give you my prayer
that you live
to pass it on.

Prodigal Blessing

May you always know
where the road home begins
and have the courage to walk the first mile.
May you never be too far from a lifeline
and never too far gone to dial.

May you know
that the God who pursues you
is a hunter whose bullets bleed mercy.
May artful accidents of grace
explode at every turn of your journey.

May you trip over truth
and fall headlong into hope.
May redemption rain down all around you.
May God's glory catch you napping
and God's story catch your breath
and God's gratuity perpetually astound you.

May choices you thought you'd made at random
turn out to be the key to moving on.
May the darkness that sometimes surrounds you
prove to be the moment before dawn.

May you bathe in the light
of a prodigal sun
and be nourished

by a generous earth.
May the struggles you meet
make you stronger
and even old wounds bring new wonders to birth.

May you trip over truth
and fall headlong into hope.
May redemption rain down all around you.
May God's glory catch you napping
and God's story catch your breath
and God's gratuity perpetually astound you.

May the unplanned kindnesses of strangers
bring to mind a long-forgotten song.
May the unexpected kisses
of a star-filled sky
remind you of where you belong.

And even if you never return to find peace
amongst those who have so loved and so hurt you,
may you seek your soul's redeemer
and connect with your creator
and make your home
with the Father who waits for you.

May you trip over truth
and fall headlong into hope.

May redemption rain down all around you.
May God's glory catch you napping
and God's story catch your breath
and God's gratuity perpetually astound you.

START IN THE HEART

Performance Notes

If spoken worship is an attempt to express in words the deepest content of a worship experience, then it follows that the poet must herself be a worshipper. The goal of spoken worship could be summed up in a single phrase: to express poetry at the heart of worship and worship in the heart of the poet. It is highly unlikely that words of true worship will flow from anything other than a worshipping heart. It is perhaps possible to cheat – to find a convenient formula and follow it, to make an 'ersatz' worship experience – but there will be no quality, no depth, and in time the activity will prove fruitless and unsatisfying, like a so-called Chippendale sideboard shaped from MDF and coloured with rubbed-in boot polish. Words, on the other hand, that flow from a heart of worship will ultimately bear fruit, even where they might lack immediate appeal.

The worship poet is called to pursue twin goals, and to pursue both equally. To pursue poetry, yes: by reading it, speaking it, studying it and seeking it out. By devouring with obsessive intensity the words of great poets who have gone before. By living with words, playing with words, experimenting with words, exploring words. The calling of a poet is a calling to craft. There are skills to be learned and honed. Like any craftsman, artist or sportsman, the poet will be rewarded for every stolen moment given over to practise and improvement. The hours spent developing the gift, poring over the work of others, mapping out the landscape of talent and performance are hours well spent. The great acting teacher Stanislavsky would insist sometimes that his students could not go home from class until they had said good night to him in fifty different voices. The golfer Gary Player, when asked if it was practise that gave him his skills or just luck, said, 'It's luck – and the more I practise, the luckier I get.' Rugby hero Jonny Wilkinson in 2003 kicked a drop goal with twenty-six seconds left to play that gave England a World Cup victory and created what the *Times* newspaper called 'a moment of sporting perfection that will become part of the fabric of our lives and part of the mythology of English life'.[4] But long before this moment, Wilkinson was known as the player who in a practise session would stay behind long after others had gone home, who would practise kicks obsessively, fanatically, seeking the point of perfection that cannot be attained by any other method. Practise may not be guaranteed to make perfect, but it gets us closer than any other road. Every craft needs to be learned, developed, improved, and the worship poet who wants to be taken seriously must take seriously this call to personal growth. Some aspects of poetry may be given as a gift to us, but little will be gained if the gift is not developed and matured. Spoken worship, like any other art, is also a craft to be learned.

But the worship poet cannot live and grow by poetry alone: she must also grow in worship. A great teacher of the early church used to tell his disciples that worshipping God was like standing on the shore by moonlight. You can see a certain distance into the waves. Beyond that you can hear the roar of their tumbling weight. But beyond both what you see and what you hear, you know that there is a vast ocean you have not even begun to explore. The worship poet stands on this very shore and points others towards the boundless depths of God, but to do so she must herself be an explorer. To shift the metaphor, she must be willing, herself, to climb the mountains she describes. If knowing God is an adventure of which we will never find an end, a journey whose joys lie before us like an invitation to the open road, if worship is a landscape to explore and a symphony to learn, then the worship poet must come with tales to tell of exploration. She must have ventured, at the very least, beyond the end of the street. Who wants to hear the songs of a sailor who has never left port? Who has time for an explorer who has never been beyond the downstairs hallway?

To be a true explorer, to have tales to tell and songs to sing, means to have gone deep in worship, to have adventured in prayer, to have allowed contemplation and meditation on the goodness of God to shape and change my thinking. I cannot help others to go together to a place I have never been alone. The essence of worship is the 'I-Thou' relationship with God; it is the business of connecting with the Creator; and the source material of spoken worship is the substance of this relationship. Unless I have such a relationship and value it above all others, what can I possibly have to say as a worship poet? Unless it is my goal to know God, how can I even begin to usher others along?

The energy I invest in my craft I must also invest in my soul. I must clamber over the face of God like a climber on Mount Rushmore. I must grow by going, discover by doing, be enlarged in my experience. I must treat worship itself, as well as the poetry I bring to it, as a craft to be learned.

The Call

In the whirlwind
of the crush-hour conflict
when movement is measured in millions
and arrival
is the only goal,

God calls to us.

In the night that settles
like snow over the city,
a blanket to smother the day,
while under the silence
those for whom sleep is no shelter
struggle to settle their souls,

God calls to us.

In the darting eyes of children
born to the ghetto of an aching need,
born to ask why longing
must always outweigh satisfaction,

God calls to us.

And when we walk
a crowded city street,
touching more people
than the human mind can count,
yet are as alone

as hermits,
when we think we go
unnoticed,

God calls to us,
"I love you."

A Marvelous Healing

For John Baker

It was a marvelous healing;
after the months of asking,
of waiting;
after the desperate, slow deterioration,
the warring tides
of faith and doubt:
to be released in an instant
from every pain.
It was as if the very molecules of his flesh
had been infused, invaded
with the life of God
until he was filled, fit to burst,
with the shalom, the peace,
of the Father's rule.
Limbs that had fallen flaccid with weakness
waved and danced with joy;
lungs that had so utterly failed him
sang out with strength and boldness.

He ran
through the unfamiliar sunlight,
drinking it in,
experiencing all at once
the thousand and one feelings
that for so long had been denied him.

It was a marvellous healing:
to be so totally restored,
made whole,
rebuilt.
It had just surprised him,
a little,
that he had had to die
to receive it.

Humanifesto

I want to be a grace guerilla,
no longer a chameleon of karma;
the time has come to stand out
from the crowd.
I want to give forgiveness
a fighting chance
of freeing me,
to live in love
and live it out loud.

I want to drink deep
of the foolishness of wisdom
instead of swallowing
the wisdom of fools,
to find a source
in the deeper mines of meaning.
I want to search out the unsearchable,
to invoke the invisible,
to choose the truths
the TV hypnotists aren't screening.

No camouflage,
no entourage,
no smoothly fitting in.
I want a faith that goes further than face value
and a beauty that goes deeper than my skin.

I want to be untouched by my possessions
instead of being possessed
by what I touch,
to test the taste
of having nothing to call mine,
to hold consumption's cravings back,
to be content with luck or lack,
to live as well on water as on wine.

I want to spend myself
on those I think might need me,
not spend
all I think I need on myself.
I want my heart
to be willing to make house calls.
Let those whose rope is at an end
find in me a faithful friend.
Let me be known as one who rebuilds broken walls.

No camouflage,
no entourage,
no smoothly fitting in.
I want a faith that goes further than face value
and a beauty that goes deeper than my skin.

I want to be centred outside the circle,
to be chiselled from a different seam.

I want to be seduced by another story
and drawn into a deeper dream,
to be anchored in an undiscovered ocean,
to revolve around an unfamiliar sun,
to be a boom box tuned to an alternate station,
a bullet fired from a different gun.

No camouflage,
no entourage,
no smoothly fitting in.
I want a faith that goes further than face value
and a beauty that goes deeper than my skin.

Healing Poem

My heart is like an iceberg:
not cold and hard
but seven-tenths hidden.
If I love you only
with the tenths that show,
my love won't last the course,
but if I am to love you with my whole heart,
I must face the pain
of hidden things
surfacing.
Come, Lord,
with the *Titanic* of your love.
Collide with my heart,
and in that great collision
let it be my reservations
that sink forever.

SAVOUR THE STORY

Performance Notes

Because it arises from, and thrives in, the worship experience, spoken worship is a literary form that is nurtured and supported through the savouring of scripture. The Christian scriptures are not a recipe book for successful living, nor a legal code for the conduct of the religious life. They are, rather, the repository of stories lived out through a hundred generations and carrying the inner dynamics of thousands of human lives pursuing the divine initiative in the world. These are the stories – this is the story – by which we are nourished in our faith and challenged in our culture.

It is of the very essence of the Christian journey that we are a storied people. Like our Jewish forefathers, we are shaped by the stories of God's actions in history. And just as the Hebrew slaves were given the enactment of the Passover and told to 'tell this to your children', so we are called to re-enact and retell the story of Jesus over and over. The great dramatic events of scripture tell the story of a God who time and again chooses grace over karma, who breaks into history to make losers winners, who chooses the ultimate act of self-emptying as the central drama of his own life. And it is significant that this story, before it was captured in prose, was a song. The words recorded in the second chapter of the apostle Paul's letter to the church of Philippi are, according to most scholars, the earliest record we have of a Christian hymn or worship song. Here are those words as given in the New Living Translation:

> Your attitude should be the same that Christ Jesus had. Though he was God, he did not demand and cling to his rights as God. He made himself nothing; he took the humble position of a slave and appeared in human form. And in human form he obediently humbled himself even further by dying a criminal's death on a cross. Because of this, God raised him up to the heights of heaven and gave him a name that is above every other name, so that at the name of Jesus every knee will bow, in heaven and on earth and under the earth, and every tongue will confess that Jesus Christ is Lord, to the glory of God the Father.[5]

Thus New Testament theology, before it was prose, was poetry. The beauty and drama of truth was sung before it was debated. Poetry is an eminently biblical way of conveying and celebrating God's story.

It follows that scripture can be an important source for the work of spoken worship. The worship poet can live in scripture, breathing in and savouring its drama and its metaphors. The roads we walk as poets may be hedged in by different images and words than our forefathers used, but they travel some similar routes. Reading scripture, both in silence and aloud, can be a great source of inspiration and ideas to the worship poet. It reminds us, over and over, of who God is, of how he acts in history, of where the pursuit of his glory might take us.

It is not that the worship poet simply rewrites scripture – though this is an exercise that has its place – but more that the poet marinated in God's story is more likely to sing in tune with it. Choosing, as a poet, to dive deep into scripture and to spend time under its waters is like learning to compose by listening to Mozart and Beethoven, like growing as an architect by walking through the buildings of Frank Lloyd Wright. It is not enough to copy, but it is wonderful to be challenged and inspired.

The story we live in was not written yesterday. It is not a recent invention. It is deep, weathered, rooted in experiences hugely older than our own. It has been lived in, tried out, offered up and written down by generations who predate us by millennia. It is a well whose waters have been tested and found wholesome over centuries of adventurous faith. Draw from it. Dive into it. Let its coolness refresh your soul. Speak as one who has drunk deep of an ancient and proven source.

Peter's Rock Song

This, then, is the rock
of which the church is made.
Crumbling chalk
tumbling
from the cliff face
of an ordinary life.
Pebbles
on an everyday shoreline,
washed by the waters
of too many passing years,
too many impetuous choices,
too many unwise moves.
When your resolve is as soft as sandstone,
it takes just a servant girl's sneer
to erode it.

Too many headstrong promises,
flecks of self-determination
firm as flint,
a stubborn streak
as gritty as granite.

All in all as flawed a block of rock
as a sculptor ever selected.

Yet deep within,
an open heart

ready to repent,
prepared to learn:
a heart of flesh,
not stone.

Strength in weakness,
freedom to fail,
softness in stone:
this, then, is the rock
of which the church is made.

When the Walls

When the walls
of Babylon are closing in
and Jerusalem
is a dim
and distant dream,
shut the door,
open a window
and pray.

When narrowness of vision
smothers hope
and stifles your every ambition,
shut the door,
open a window
and pray.

When you need to find your focus
in a free and far horizon
and to see beyond the furniture
that frames you,
shut the door,
open a window
and pray.

When darkness encroaches
and shadows fight with sight
and you crave the comfort of light,

shut the door,
open a window
and pray.

When the presence of God is a misted memory
and the promises of God are slow in coming
and the purposes of God are buried in the fields of your
    anxiety,
when you are stuck,
stagnated,
struggling,
without hope
and without help in the world,

shut the door
in the presence of your Father,
open a window
to the promise of your redeemer
and pray
to the one who loves and lives
for you
and longs to help you
more than you can ever know.

In the Image of My Father

Made in the image of my Father:
breath-filled,
his will to live kindling my life,
his call to be driving my being.
My heart is sparked by his heart;
my mind is fired by his imagination.
My animation is his declaration:
because he is, I am.

Made in the image of my Father:
able,
artful, articulate,
created to create,
pulsing with potential.
Designed to design,
invented for invention,
made to make.
Through his eyes, I see possibilities.
Through his ears, I hear harmonies.
In his heartbeat, I feel life's dancing rhythms.
Because he can,
I will.

Made in the image of my Father:
dependent,
rooted in relationship,
commissioned for companionship,
a free individual made free in community,

distinct yet needing devotion,
complete but needing completion.
Unique, I seek the company of others.
A part, I seek my meaning in the whole.
Because of him, I need to be needed.
Because I am loved, I love.

Made in the image of my Father:
human,
his word of command shaping flesh,
his loving intention sculpting the soil of earth into life.
His voice causing, calling, claiming me, naming me,
framing my future,
fashioning me.
Because of his dreams, I have promise.
Because of his promise, I have dreams.

Ushered into extravagant existence,
tumbling into time,
fumbling,
falling,
free.
I am human.
I am dependent.
I am able.
I am breath-filled.
I am made
in the image of my Father.

The Very Thought

I love the very thought of heaven,
where angels sing
in perfect, perpetual choir practice,
where Father, Son and Spirit rule
unchallenged
and are honoured in full measure.

I love the very thought of heaven,
but I was not made
to live there.
I was not made
to walk on clouds
and bask eternally
in immaterial splendour.

I was made for this green planet,
this tight ball
of aching beauty
alive with the unending possibilities
of his creative power.

I was made for the sunshine
that blazes through the veins of a leaf
and glints on the tiny, perfect back
of a ladybird crossing my arm.
I was made to be human
in this most human of places.

I was made for earth;
the earth is my home.

That's why I'm glad that God,
more than anyone,
is a friend of the earth,
prepared as he was to die
for its redemption,
and that's why I'm glad
that the magnificent, jewelled foundations
of the mighty pearly gates
will be anchored
deeply and forever
in the soil of earth.

Harold Be Your Name

Hallowed be your name,
for you are *Frank*
with us and firm in your forgiveness.
When the junk of sin
so tangled in our nets
must be cut free,
hallowed be your name.

Hallowed be your name,
for you are *Jasper*
in our poverty
and *Beryl*
to our sand,
and you are *Ruby*
in the clay pots of our lives.
Hallowed be your name.

Hallowed be your name,
for you are *Justin*
all your ways, and true,
and *Patience* is your nature.
We have *Faith* in your fullness,
we learn
from your *Earnest* love.
Hallowed be your name.

Hallowed be your name,
for you *Mark* us with your love

and *Carrie* us
through every shadowed valley,
and wherever *Hugo*,
we will run to follow,
for in the *Nick* of time,
on the very *Eve* of eternity,
saved by the *Belle*,
we will glory in the triumph
of your *Grace*.
Hallowed be your name.

This God

This God,
who watches worlds,
sees my heart.
This careful calculator,
counting countless millions,
counts me in.
This artist,
whose canvass outstretches
eternity at both ends,
whose palette out-shines planets,
paints my portrait.
This lover,
who dreams in universes,
dreams of me.
This creator,
whose breadth of vision spans time
and spawns a cosmos,
whose woven tapestry of purpose,
more compound than chaos,
eclipsing complexity,
rolls out like a highway through history,
whose heartbeat deafens supernovas,
this perfect parent
kisses me.
This playwright,
playing

with the deaths and entrances of stars,
scripting
the end from the beginning,
knowing
the purpose of the play,
watches my feeble audition,
and writes
me
in.

Psalm Enchanted Evening

Performance Notes

The most obvious source of spoken worship in scripture is the Psalms – the hymn book of the Hebrew people over generations of their development and growth. And if there are lessons to be learned from the Psalms, one amongst them must be the truth that worship cannot all be sugarcoated. Jonny Baker says of these age-old songs of worship and lament:

> The Psalms have been read and reread to give comfort, hope and encouragement all over the world down through the centuries. It is an amazing thing that these songs and poems have this enduring character. Perhaps one of the reasons for this is that they are gritty and real. A lot of Christian worship songs can be unrealistic in their positive outlook, censoring voices of darkness and disorientation. But most of us simply don't experience life that way, at least not all of the time. Even if our own lives are going well and we sense the joy of life and God's presence, one glance at a newspaper is enough to remind us that a lot of people in the world face very difficult situations of war, poverty and oppression. What a relief to have the honesty of the Psalms in the Bible![6]

There is no simplistic escapism in the Psalms: they have life precisely because they are so real. They are prepared to deal with the shadow as with the light, with real emotions of fear, disappointment and betrayal. There is anguish here, and loss. If hope is the consistent undertone of scripture, it is a tone carried under both joy and confusion, both triumph and tragedy. Hope is rooted in who God is not in how things are for those of us who are seeking him. The landscapes of our lives can be as filled with distress as with delight, with helplessness as with happiness, but in either case we are called to look to the horizon. Our help comes from the God who watches over us, who waits to bless us, who sends a cloud no bigger than a man's fist, then taps us on the shoulder to say, 'Look!' It is not the circumstances we stand in that dictate our joy but the direction we face, not where we are situated but how we respond.

The psalmists understand this. They call us, from wherever we stand, to look to God. They draw our eyes to the divine, to the eternal faithfulness of God, to the one who is good and whose love endures forever.

Thus spoken worship, as a contemporary psalmody, does not seek to paint a picture of a saccharine world of carefree joy in which all is wonderful and no shadow falls. Rather, it throws light on the real world in which suffering lives next door to satisfaction and pain shares airspace with pleasure, and yet in which hope triumphs. This is the faith of the Psalms – not hope instead of reality but hope in the face of reality. Spoken worship has the power to affirm that in all the suffering and ugliness of the world, there is a God of beauty yet to be found.

U2 frontman, Bono, in his 1999 introduction to the Psalms in the Canongate Scriptures series, says:

> Years ago, lost for words and with 40 minutes of recording time left before the end of our studio time, we were still looking for a song to close our third album, *War*. We wanted to put something explicitly spiritual on the record to balance the politics and romance of it; like Bob Marley or Marvin Gaye would. We thought about the psalms – Psalm 40. There was some squirming. We were a very "white" rock group, and such plundering of the scriptures was taboo for a white rock group unless it was in the "service of Satan." Psalm 40 is interesting in that it suggests a time in which grace will replace karma, and love will replace the very strict laws of Moses (in other words, fulfil them). I love that thought. David, who committed some of the most selfish as well as selfless acts, was depending on it. That the scriptures are brim full of hustlers, murderers, cowards, adulterers and mercenaries used to shock me. Now it is a source of great comfort. "40" became the closing song at U2 shows, and on hundreds of occasions, literally hundreds of thousands of people of every size and shape of T-shirt have shouted back the refrain, pinched from Psalm 6: "How long (to sing this song)." I had thought of it as a

nagging question, pulling at the hem of an invisible deity whose presence we glimpse only when we act in love. How long hunger? How long hatred? How long until creation grows up and the chaos of its precocious, hell-bent adolescence has been discarded? I thought it odd that the vocalising of such questions could bring such comfort – to me, too.[7]

How might the worship lives of churches and the devotional lives of believers in the twenty-first century be revolutionised by a generation of poets who rediscover the 'hope and reality' worldview of the Psalms? What Psalms are there, still waiting to be written, still waiting to be spoken, for worshippers in search of the authentic voice of faith in the real world?

23 Not Out

God is my home-help,
my companion,
my full-time carer.
All that I need
that I can't provide,
he brings to me.

Like a guide dog
a route map,
a satellite guidance system,
he gets me
to where I need to be.

Like a herdsman,
a shepherd,
a cowboy,
a game-park warden,
he sees to it that I reach
good grazing.
He has a nose for the freshest water,
an eye for the greenest grass.

He's the headmaster
I want to spend time with,
the constable
whose company I don't fear.

He watches my back,
keeps me covered,
keeps me free
to be me.

When the things I most dread
press in on me,
when death
and debt
and sickness
fall like shadows across my path,
he lets me know he's there:
a pinch in the darkness,
a poke in the ribs,
a whisper in my ear,
a slap in the face of fear,
and I press on
until shadow gives way to sun.

My goodness!
I'm being followed.
Mercy me!
I'm being tailed.
And, stalker and all,
I intend to live like this
forever.

You Catch My Eye

You catch my eye
in the eye of the storm.
You hold ointment appointments
when hell's hornets swarm.
When I find no time for stillness,
you tell me there's still time.
When my words are clashing symbols,
you are reason,
rhythm,
rhyme.
You are the song that rises
in my soul,
the coin that clatters
in my begging bowl.
You're a bed of roses on a crowded street,
a peppermint balm to my blistered feet.
You are rich in rest
when rest is radium-rare.
By cool pools you position me.
With passion you petition me.
In fog and smog,
you recondition my air.
You are the unexpected cheer
that lifts my game.
In the vinegar and lemon juice of life,
you are champagne.

Like honey on the throat to Frank Sinatra,
Like a goat's-milk bath to Cleopatra,
you surround me to astound me,
you soothe and smooth.
You are the stalker
who is good for me,
the jailer
who can set me free,
the trap and snare
to bind me into love.
You who have refined me,
come find me,
mind me,
by grace grind me
and bind me,
gentle jailer,
into love.

God Spell

Arrest me, oh God, until I am free.
Blind me until the scales fall from my eyes.
Cajole me, corral me, confront what's soft in me,
God of comfort, who will never compromise.

Divorce me, my God, from all that harms my heart.
Extend me beyond my feeble dreams.
Fix me, firm and fast, to your unfolding future,
God of visions, who is not what he may seem.

Glue me, great God, in the grip of your goodness.
Hold me in the harbour of your hand.
Infuse me, inspire me, invest in my perfection,
God of grace I will not always understand.

Jump-start me, jolting God, when my ignition fails me.
Kick me into life when life is waiting.
Leapfrog my reluctance, lead me in your dance,
God of sacrifice, on whose thin ice I am skating.

Mark me, wounded God, with the subtle bruise of love.
Needle me with needs that crave compassion.
Outrage my inhibitions, overrule my cold inaction,
God of giving, who will not grant me isolation.

Provoke me, powerful God, to a panoramic vision.
Question me when I excuse my small ambitions.

Reason with me, read intentions, renew my once-strong dreams,
God of instincts far beyond imagination.

Scorch me, searing God, when my temperature is falling.
Traumatise me when my spirit is sedated.
Upset my dull routines, undermine my oversleeping,
God of wildfire, who will not be domesticated.

Vaccinate me, holy God, against the selfish gene's encroachment.
Wash the self-inflicted wounds of my false feelings.
X-ray my heart until every motive shows,
God of hygiene, holding out for my full healing.

Yearn for me, God of love, whose very life is longing.
Zero in on every fault line I've befriended,
Zoom in on my mind-maps,
Zone out my danger zones,
God of endings, who will leave no song unended.

SEASONING FOR THE SEASONS

Performance Notes

One of the areas in which spoken worship can most effectively contribute to the corporate or liturgical life of a community of faith is through its capacity to mark and celebrate the seasons: of life itself and of the church year. There are moments in every life – birth, marriage and death are the big three, but there are many others depending on your background, community and local situation – that need to be marked by more than a shrug of the shoulders and a red circle on the calendar. They call for ritual, for the speaking of shared memory, for moments of space and silence. Spoken worship can fulfil a crucial role in marking these moments. Poetry can play its part in the welcoming of a newborn child, in the celebration of a marriage, in the bittersweet remembering of those we have loved and lost. Something about the depth of these moments is already beyond rational language and lives by definition in the poetic realm. It is at the most significant moments in the life of the tribe that the services of the bard are most called for.

What is true of the journey we make 'between the forceps and the stone' is also true of the path we tread, with comforting familiarity, through each year. It may not be easy to find new words at Christmas and Easter, but it is worth trying to do so. These are shared moments of identity and wonder, moments when we ask life-testing questions, when we check our meanings and motivations and are open to change. They are moments when the skilled wordsmith can articulate what many others are thinking but struggle to say. We celebrate such 'holy days' precisely because they offer us a shared experience: they punctuate our lives with shafts of insight that go beyond the personal, that connect to one another and, quite possibly, to something or someone beyond.

It is often at such moments that the boundaries separating poetry from prophecy and prayer are most blurred. Are the words of hope spoken over a child who has been brought for christening or dedication poetic or prophetic? Are the memories of a dear friend gathered from the dust and made beautiful at the moment of burial poetry or prayer? What of the passion and joy spoken over a couple coming together in marriage?

Or the words offered to a community gathered to mark the coming of another Christmas? It is often difficult to know, in such places, whether words are literary or liturgical, whether the speaker stands as poet or as priest. Very often both are true, and there is a raw and tangible power in the coming together of art and aspiration. In either case, we offer our words as worship. Like the bread and wine that are set apart to become something more, so the words that begin their lives as simple sentences and phrases, that are ink on a page and dots of light on a screen, that pass through the vibration of vocal cords to hang like birds in the silence of a solemn moment become, just possibly, something more than the sum of the letters that have formed them.

In a world that has trivialised the celebration of the passing seasons, that has commercialised every conceivable corporate occasion, that seeks to sentimentalise the shared moments of birth and marriage and even of death, spoken worship can serve to bring reality back into our rituals and depth back into our lives. It has a high and holy calling and carries within itself the potential to help even the most hardened cynic to mark, in some small way, the wonder of life.

Christmas Is Waiting

Christmas is waiting to happen.
Outside, a vacant hillside
lies silent, strangely empty
of any angel's choir.
A stable waits
for bookings at the inn to multiply.
Distant kings study charts
and keep gifts in cold storage,
while shepherds plan their memoirs
in expectancy of unexpected fame
and keep a chapter free
for miracles.
A small velvet patch
in the black night sky
stands ready to hold a newborn star,
and oppressed peoples everywhere
cling wildly to prophecy and song
and whisper the word: Messiah.
They've switched on the lights
in Oxford Street,
counting off the buying days.
Like Guardsmen on parade,
shops are stocked and standing by,
revving up the engines
of their debt-powered swiping machines,
and history watchers mark another year
in the slow count to 3000.

But here an old man lies
in the stairwell where he fell three days ago
and no one knows.
Here a young girl loiters
in a streetlight's unholy halo
to sell the only thing she owns
that men will pay for.
And here an infant sleeps
on a sack on the hard earth floor
where even a mother's hand
is empty,
and there are places where Christmas
is still waiting
to happen.

Behold, I Stand

When the night is deep
with the sense of Christmas
and expectancy hangs heavy
on every breath,
behold, I stand at the door and knock.

When the floor is knee-deep
in discarded wrapping paper
and the new books are open at page one
and the new toys are already broken,
behold, I stand at the door and knock.

When the family is squashed
elbow to elbow
around the table,
and the furious rush for food is over
and the only word that can describe the feeling
is *full*,
behold, I stand at the door and knock.

When Christmas is over
and the television is silent
for the first time in two days
and who sent which card to whom
is forgotten until next year,
behold, I stand at the door.

And when the nation has finished celebrating
Christmas without Christ,
a birthday without a birth,
the coming of a kingdom
without a king,
when I am forgotten,
despised,
rejected,
crucified,
behold, I stand.

Because He Is Risen: A Poem for Easter

Because he is risen,
spring is possible
in all the cold hard places
gripped by winter
and freedom jumps the queue
to take fear's place
as our focus.
Because he is risen.

Because he is risen,
my future is an epic novel
where once it was a mere short story.
My contract on life is renewed
in perpetuity.
My options are open-ended;
my travel plans are cosmic.
Because he is risen.

Because he is risen,
healing is on order and assured
and every disability will bow
before the endless dance of his ability
and my grave too will open
when my life is restored,
for this frail and fragile body
will not be the final word
on my condition.
Because he is risen.

Because he is risen,
hunger will go begging in the streets
for want of a home
and selfishness will have a shortened shelf-life
and we will throng to the funeral of famine
and dance on the callous grave of war
and poverty will be history
in our history.
Because he is risen.

And because he is risen,
a fire burns in my bones
and my eyes see possibilities
and my heart hears hope
like a whisper on the wind
and the song that rises in me
will not be silenced
as life disrupts
this shadowed place of death
like a butterfly under the skin
and death itself
runs terrified to hide.
Because he is risen.

Dedication

For Daniel

Out of your sweetness,
may strength come forth.
In weakness,
may a brave heart grow.
In your dependence,
may faith take root.
From wide-eyed wonder,
may wisdom flow.
May the lions you face meet a warrior.
May you dance on the high fields of praise.
May rejoicing run like a river
through the valleys of your days.
May you stand in your inheritance
and live as a child of the king.
May your ears be tuned to angels
in the wind-whispered glory they sing.
May you carry a furnace fire of hope
when the world falls dark around you.
May you find in your heart
forgiveness
when others, unthinking, hurt you.
May you know
as deep as DNA
in the marrow of your soul

you are known,
you are loved,
you are valued.
Though you fear it, you are never alone.
May you walk in the cool of the evening
in the garden your maker has given.
May you bring to trembling, fragile earth
the certain touch of heaven.
May your eyes never lose the wonder
of the miracle of your birth.
From your heart, come love.
From your life, come truth.
From your sweetness,
may strength come forth.

Breadsong

It's not in the bread
but in the breaking
that the mystery of God's story is told.
It's not in the seed
but in the dying,
not in the treasure
but in the digging for it.
It's not in the mountain
but in its moving.

It's not in the wine
but in the pouring out
that a new world is purchased
for the weary.
It's not in the cross
but in the crucified,
not in the nails
but in the nailing.
It's not in the grave
but in the rising from it.

It's in the giving
that the gift becomes life;
it's in the living
that the Word becomes flesh.

It's in this taking,
this receiving,
this sharing of a supper,
this pointing to a future
that is promised
and paid for
and pressed into our hands;
it's in this everyday mealtime miracle
that the universe is born
to new life.

Emmaus Wedding

May this marriage be a milestone
on your shared road to Emmaus,
where two travel
but three share the ride.
May God himself occupy
the third seat on your tandem
as back-seat driver,
powerful pedaller, trusted guide.

May each memory you make
point to his presence,
a mystery figure
found in every frame.
May each joy you share
be a sharing of his pleasure,
each name you speak
an echo of his name.

May worship be the well
whose waters heal you,
a thread sewn through
the fabric of each day.
May his whispered voice join yours
in conversation,
his casting vote
unite you as you pray.

May you pursue the path
your partnership is made for,
the priceless pearl
of finding God's direction;
two destinations woven
in one purpose, two destinies
fulfilled in shared intention.

And as you walk together
through cool evenings
in the garden that his love
will shape and give you,
may you sense a silent presence
and feel a loving gaze
and thrill to turn
to find him walking with you.

Wedding Song

Come and share my waterbed.
Let's set sail
on a bright love's buoyancy.
We'll splash and surf
in the surging seas
of exuberant monogamy.

Scurrying towards sleep for shelter
from the fury
of the surface world's schemes,
we'll dive down deep
to where dolphins
will sing to us in our dreams.

When winter winds and power cuts
find us sleeping
on a block of ice,
we'll fashion an igloo
of our intimacy
and huddle
in a breath-warmed paradise.

And if our love should spring a leak,
then we'll work
'til we've plugged the drip,
but we won't see our hopes proved hollow
and we won't
abandon ship.

Passion's tides may ebb and flow
and our calm seas
may be rocked by harsh weather,
but come and share
my waterbed
and we'll sail through it all
together.

MYSTERY MAKING

Performance Notes

One of the basic assumptions we make about life is that words explain things. When we visit a museum, we will often be faced with a strange and intricate display. Unrecognisable objects will fill the glass cases before us, confusing us with their colours and complexities. Words come to our rescue. Little labels pinned to the right parts, commentaries that talk us through the whole, guidebooks, articles, signs and posters. Words have a vital function in taking the mystery out of our surroundings. And we are grateful that they do. Some of us know what it means to be lost for words. Do we realise, as often, that we would be lost without words?

In worship we often use words in this same way. People of faith tend to believe that others around them are asking questions, and that it is incumbent upon them – as those who believe in something – to offer answers. Like white-coated scientists extolling the glories of washing powder, we furrow our brows in professorial intensity and utter the words that will make everything clear. Truth, we believe, should be understandable, accessible, open to analysis and, above all, to explanation. The plain truth. The simple truth. True truth. The function of words in our lives is to make things clearer, to solve mysteries, to offer explanations.

But what if truth were not willing to be so tamed? What if truth, having a life and a will of its own, resisted our attempts to capture and hold it and kept wriggling away just when we thought we had it? What if the word *truth* did not refer at all to a disembodied package of concepts and ideas but pointed rather to a person, a person who might choose at will to show himself or hide from us or to lead us in a merry game of cosmic hide-and-seek? What if the mystery of it all were part of the adventure, calling us and leading us 'farther up and farther in' into ever deeper realms of exploration? If this were so, then we would need words not to solve everything but rather to point us to the next clue. Like a trail of bread crumbs left for us through the wilds of the forest, words would be markers on our journey, not points of arrival. What if words were not to solve all the mysteries at all but served rather to point deeper into their beauty?

Brian McLaren suggests that this contrast in the ways words are used is part of a significant, larger transition by which our culture is calling for subtler forms of communication:

> Our words will seek to be servants of mystery, not removers of it as they were in the old world. They will convey a message that is clear yet mysterious, simple yet mysterious, substantial yet mysterious. My faith developed in the old world of many words, in a naïve confidence in the power of many words, as if the mysteries of faith could be captured like fine-print conditions in a legal document and reduced to safe equations. Mysteries, however, can not be captured so precisely. Freeze-dried coffee, butterflies on pins and frogs in formaldehyde all lose something in our attempts at capturing, defining, preserving and rendering them less jumpy, flighty or fluid. In the new world, we will understand this a little better.[8]

If McLaren is right, then worship is one of the areas in which there is the most work to be done in reshaping and deepening the way words are used. We will need fewer neat phrases to close a line of enquiry and more rich metaphors to open others, less 'simple truth' and more 'deep beauty'. We will need words that intrigue and attract, that sparkle and glisten with the promise of new discoveries, words that invite their hearers to look deeper and travel farther.

Poetry is not just a 'prettier' way of saying the same old things. It is not verbal wallpaper designed to make our lives feel better. It is an invitation to a journey, a challenge to a deeper life. Its words are wingless angels sent to stir the souls of men and women and to lift their eyes to the farthest horizons of hope that imagination can make possible.

The worship poet should not be afraid to invoke mystery, to engender awe and wonder. Her goal should not be to render all things understandable so much as to declare all things beautiful. Where there is mess and contradiction and paradox and perplexity in the everyday flow of human experience, worship is not there to iron out the difficulties and make it all seem simple. It is there to ask the question, 'Where is God in this?' It holds up the realities of the complex lives we lead, of our frailties and failures, of the questions that even after years of asking remain obstinately unresolved, and it says, 'Where is beauty?' It holds on with one hand to the power and majesty of the Creator and with the other to the pain of his world, and it cries, 'I won't let go.' Spoken worship doesn't set out to simplify, to reduce and resolve, to explain. Its currency is wonder, its fuel beauty. The current that runs through it is the current of love, explored and delivered in the mud and grime of a world derailed by our dysfunctions.

> Then perchance comes the power of poetry – shattering, evocative speech that breaks fixed conclusions and presses us always toward new, dangerous, imaginative possibilities.[9]

Eight

God, you're so big.
Bigger than Beckham.
Bigger than Wal-Mart.
Bigger than the Taj Mahal.
When I look into the depths of you,
I see there is no end of you,
and I wonder that you think of me at all.

You reach farther out than Hubble,
deeper in than Loch Ness;
you whisper louder than
the roaring of the sea.
And when I look into the depths of you
and see there is no end of you,
I wonder what it is you see in me.

When I try to measure you,
I can't find words enough for you
or concepts that can capture you
or hold more than a hint of you.
You are an eel that slips away from me,
a distant sigh that calls to me,
a beauty always just beyond embrace.
And when I look into the depths of you
and see there is no end of you,
I wonder why you've given me this place.

You've set me just below the stars,
two steps from an angel choir.
You've laid the world and all its wonders out before me,
and when I look into the depths of you,
I see there is no end of you,
and the truth that trips and teases me,
like a tingling tooth that troubles me,
when having faith in you so stretches me
is the miracle
that you should have
such faith in me.

This Grace

This grace we have been given is enough.
When the mountains set before us
won't move by faith
until by faith we start to climb,
it is enough.
When our cry for heaven's miracles
rings hollow,
like a doorbell howling through an empty house,
it is enough.

When from our waiting rooms of weakness
we say yes
to pressing on,
it is enough.
When we have reached the end of our energies
and face the end of ourselves
but can't yet see the end of our task,
it is enough.

Enough
to know that you have loved us.
Enough
that we are called before all time.
Enough
that every fingerprint is valued.
Enough
that you remember every name.

So we will embrace this grace
and turn our hearts to face grace.
Loosening the locks
on our personal space,
we'll make each home a place of grace.
We'll drink from your wells
'til we're wasted on grace;
we'll speak out your words
'til our tongues taste of grace.
And we'll live to love your laws
until our lives are laced with grace.

Down dark and dingy alleys
we will chase grace.
We will hold as something precious every trace of grace.
We will celebrate and consecrate this grace,
because this grace we have been given
is enough.

Poetic Justice (Because
Laughter Is Worship Too)

Supermarket trolley, oh supermarket trolley,
discarded and forgotten like an outdated song,
do you remember the time when,
chrome-bright and jolly,
you danced like a dodgem
through the fruit-weighing throng?
I know some would accuse me of sentimental folly,
but I'm sad
to see the drowning
of a supermarket trolley.
Your mesh is enmeshed now with river weed and slime,
and the letters on your handle
are irreversibly smudged,
and though I could simply say
that you've fallen on hard times,
it gives me unexpected pleasure
to believe you're being judged
for all those times when in some crowded aisle or other
I pushed you one way
and your wheels
went another.

Notes

1. Henry Wadsworth Longfellow, 'Tegner's Drapa', accessed at *www.pitt.edu/~dash/longfellow.html#tegner*, August 4, 2006.

2. Walter Brueggemann, *Finally Comes the Poet: Daring Speech for Proclamation* (Minneapolis: Fortress, 1989), 3.

3. Ibid.

4. Simon Barnes, 'Wilkinson and the Making of a Myth', *Times Online*, November 24, 2003.

5. Phil. 2:5–11 NLT.

6. Jonny Baker, *Redemption Songs in Daily Bread* (Milton Keynes: Scripture Union, 2003).

7. Bono, 'Introduction to the Psalms', in *The Book of Psalms*, The Canongate Scriptures (Edinburgh: Canongate, 1999).

8. Brian D. McLaren, *The Church on the Other Side: Doing Ministry in the Postmodern Matrix* (Grand Rapids, MI: Zondervan, 2000), 89.

9. Brueggemann, *Finally Comes the Poet*, 6.

Gerard Kelly is senior pastor of Crossroads International Church in Amsterdam, The Netherlands, and a founding trustee of the Bless Network, a UK-based mission organisation working with churches on mainland Europe. He was for ten years a member of the leadership team of the UK teaching event Spring Harvest, where his worship poetry has been a significant feature over a number of years. Gerard's poems have been used on BBC radio and television, are regularly featured in Christian gatherings large and small in the UK and in the USA, and have been included in both the *Lion Collection of Christian Poetry* and the *Young Oxford Book of Christmas Verse*. Gerard is married to Chrissie, and they have four children at various stages of childhood, youth and adulthood.

We want to hear from you. Please send your comments about this book to us in care of zreview@zondervan.com. Thank you.

ZONDERVAN.com/
AUTHORTRACKER
follow your favorite authors